THE SPACE EXPLORER'S GUIDE TO

Great Cosmic Questions

BY
RACHEL CONNOLLY

WITH
RYAN WYATT
VISUAL ADVISOR

AND
JIM SWEITZER, PH.D.
NASA SCIENCE CENTER,
DePAUL UNIVERSITY

SCHOLASTIC INC.

NEW YORK TORONTO LONDON AUCKLAND SYDNEY
MEXICO CITY NEW DELHI HONG KONG BUENOS AIRES

Who's Who at Space U

Rachel Connolly
Writer
Rachel manages the astrophysics education program at the American Museum of Natural History's Rose Center for Earth and Space.

Ryan Wyatt
Visual Advisor
Ryan designs scientific visuals for the American Museum of Natural History's Rose Center for Earth and Space.

Jim Sweitzer
Advisor
Jim is an astrophysicist and the director of the NASA Space Science Center at DePaul University in Chicago.

With special thanks to:
Dr. Maulik Parikh, Dr. Justin Khoury, and Dr. Rocky Kolb

ISBN: 0-439-55749-6

Copyright © 2004 by Scholastic Inc.

Editor: Andrea Menotti
Assistant Editor: Megan Gendell
Designers: Peggy Gardner, Lee Kaplan, Tricia Kleinot
Illustrators: Diana Fitter, Yancey C. Labat, Thomas Nakid, Ed Shems

Photos:
All photos by NASA and the Hubble Heritage Team (STScI/AURA) unless otherwise noted.
Front cover: A spiral galaxy known as the Sombrero Galaxy
Back cover: A nebula in the constellation Orion known as NGC 1999
Title page: A spiral galaxy called NGC 4622

Pages 8 and 21: (CMB) NASA/WMAP Science Team. Page 9: (Lemaitre) Science Photo Library/Photo Researchers; (Hubble) Sanford Roth/Photo Researchers; (large spiral galaxy) NOAO/AURA/NSF. Pages 9, 15, 46, and 48: (Hubble Ultra Deep Field) NASA, ESA, S. Beckwith (STScI) and the HUDF Team. Page 14: (Earth) NASA/R. Stöckli/Robert Simmon/GSFC/MODIS. Page 16: (Leavitt) Harvard College Observatory/Photo Researchers; (Hubble) Hale Observatories/Photo Researchers; (spiral galaxy) N.A. Sharp/NOAO/AURA/NSF; (Cepheid Variable star) Dr. Wendy L. Freedman/Observatories of the Carnegie Institution of Washington/NASA. Page 20: Lucent Technologies Inc./Bell Labs. Page 21: (WMAP) NASA/WMAP Science Team. Page 23: (Tevatron views) Fermilab photo; (particle tracks) CERN Geneva. Page 27: Courtesy of the Archives, California Institute of Technology. Page 31, 35, and 36: (Earth) NASA. Page 34: (young Einstein) Albert Einstein Archives/The Hebrew University of Jerusalem; (older Einstein) Library of Congress/Oren Jack Turner. Page 35: (news story) The New York Times, November 10, 1919. Page 37 (bottom): NASA/CXC/M. Weiss. Page 41: (Rubin) Courtesy of Dr. Vera Rubin. Page 42: (Hubble) NASA; (Abell cluster) NASA, Andrew Fruchter and the ERO Team [Sylvia Baggett (STScI), Richard Hook (ST-ECF), Zoltan Levay (STScI)] (STScI). Page 44: photos courtesy of Dr. Rocky Kolb. Page 46: (top blue spiral) NASA, The Hubble Heritage Team and A. Riess (STScI); Page 47: (LISA) NASA/JPL; (LHC) CERN Geneva; (James Webb) Northrop Grumman Space Technology.

12 11 10 9 8 7 6 5 4 3 2 1   4 5 6 7 8 9/0

Printed in the U.S.A.

First Scholastic printing, July 2004

The publisher has made every effort to ensure that the activities in this book are safe when done as instructed. Adults should provide guidance and supervision whenever the activity requires.

Table of **Contents**

JOIN THE HUNT FOR

C adet, are you ready to investigate some of the biggest mysteries in the universe? Ready to jump in and explore some of the weirdest, wildest, most cosmically cool stuff out there? Now's your chance!

This month, you'll feast your mind on **great cosmic questions** like these:

■ How do we know the universe began with a BIG BANG?

■ What is space?

■ What is time?

■ How are space and time related?

■ How does space get *warped*?

■ Is time travel possible?

■ What are worm holes?

HEY! Where'd you go?

I'm over here!

■ How might the universe someday, in the far-distant future, come to an end?

If these questions get your brain all fired up, then you'll love the science of *cosmology.*

WHAT IS COSMOLOGY?

Cosmology is a science that studies the **universe as a whole.** Here's where the name comes from:

COSMOS	+	OLOGY	= COSMOLOGY
This word means "an orderly system." It's the opposite of *chaos,* which means "mess."		This ending means "the study of something."	

Cosmologists are the detectives of the universe. They're hot on the trail of clues to solve some of the biggest mysteries of science, like how our universe got started and what its future will hold.

You, cadet, are now an apprentice to these cosmic sleuths! This book will introduce you to four great cases, and you'll meet four master detectives who'll guide you on your cosmic clue hunt:

Detective Hugh Niverse lights the way in *The Case of the Big Bang* (see page 7).

Detective Lotte DeMension unfolds *The Case of Space and Time* (see page 24).

Detective Ivana B. Hidden investigates *The Case of the Missing Matter* (see page 40).

Detective Barry Distant takes on *The Case of the Cosmic Conclusion* (see page 45).

With help from your guides, you'll discover the clues you need to piece together the great puzzles of the universe!

A GOLDEN AGE

Right now, cosmology is in a really special time of growth and discovery—many are calling it a "golden age." There are lots of reasons for this, but great new tools are the *biggest* reason. Bigger and better telescopes and faster computers mean that scientists can find all sorts of clues, and they can test out their ideas with lots of experiments. You'll notice, cadet, that many of the discoveries in this book were made pretty recently—some even during *your* lifetime!

Being in a "golden age" means that what we know about the universe is changing and growing very fast. It's like we're putting together a huge puzzle without knowing what it will look like in the end—so we often find pieces that don't make sense to us…YET!

So, cadet, are you ready to join forces with the cosmic sleuths and get *clued in* to the mysteries of the universe? Then turn to page 7 to start your first case…with a big BANG!

WHAT'S IN THIS MONTH'S SPACE CASE?

This month's Space Case is full of cool tools to help you on your cosmic quest. You've got:

■ **A space-time fabric grid.** This cosmic canvas stretches and warps like the real universe! To see it in action, head over to page 32 at warp speed!

■ **One large ball and one small one.** Use this pair with your space-time fabric grid to create cool warps and orbits!

■ **A cosmic balloon.** Expand your horizons with your very own glow-in-the-dark, galaxy-spotted universe! To see what the universe and a balloon have in common, *blow* over to page 18!

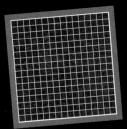

Glowing galaxies to stick on your balloon

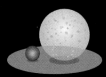

■ **A metal spring.** Use this coil to model your own light waves! Spring to page 11 to get started!

THE SPACE UNIVERSITY WEB SITE

As always, more fun awaits you on the Space U web site (www.scholastic.com/space). You can see a black hole in action, make your own space-time warps, and more! Just make sure to bring along this month's password!

You know the drill, cadet! Complete your web missions to earn your latest patch. Then paste it right here!

PLANET PASSWORD
This month's web site password is:
COSMICQUEST

BANG!

All the ingredients that would eventually make up you, the planets, the stars, the galaxies, the book you're holding, and everything else in the universe burst forth 13.7 billion years ago in an utterly enormous eruption of energy.

The Big Bang is the name given to this great cosmic expansion. How it all happened is one of the greatest puzzles that cosmologists have ever grappled with.

The early universe was a hot, thick fog of particles and light!

...BUT WHAT BANGED?

If this question is on your mind, cadet, you are not alone! But unfortunately, **the Big Bang theory does *not* have an answer for you!**

The theory can tell you what happened a tiny fraction of a second *after* the "bang," but it cannot describe the bang itself—that's where the laws of physics break down. In fact, the name "Big Bang" was originally given to this theory as a joke, but the name stuck. Who knows if "bang" is really the right word to describe what happened!

THE WHOLE SHE BANG!

The Big Bang is really a way to describe how the early universe grew and aged, from being very small and hot to being much larger and cooler. The Big Bang theory doesn't say exactly *how* or *why* the BANG happened, and it doesn't explain what the universe might have been like *before* it went BANG!

Anyone can think about these big questions and come up with their own ideas, but unless you can test your ideas with an experiment, it's not science—it's just a guess or "speculation."

But who knows, cadet, maybe someday you'll find a way to test your ideas and answer those big, brain-boggling questions with science!

THE HISTORY OF THE UNIVERSE

Less than a second!   380,000 years

The Big Bang

With the Big Bang, all the energy in the universe burst forth, creating matter and stretching space itself in all directions. The stretching is still going on today!

The Big Bang was not an explosion like the kind you see in movies, where things get hurled through space. In this big eruption of energy, space *itself* was created and unfurled in all directions!

Tiny Particles Form

Still within the first second after the BANG, the first tiny particles—electrons, protons, and neutrons—began to form. This went on for about three minutes. During this time, the universe was a hot, thick fog. Light bounced wildly around among the particles, trapped in the crowd.

proton ———————
neutron ———————
electron ———————

Particles Link Up

After a few minutes, protons and neutrons began to stick together. These linked particles would later become the centers of atoms, mostly hydrogen and helium atoms.

When we measure the amounts of hydrogen and helium found in our universe today, the amounts we find give us solid evidence that the Big Bang really happened. To check out this important clue, turn to page 22!

 center of hydrogen atom

 center of helium atom

Atoms Form, Light Escapes!

After about 380,000 years, the universe had expanded and cooled enough to allow the linked protons and neutrons to become complete atoms, with electrons orbiting around them. Before this, it was just too hot for the protons and neutrons to hang on to the excited electrons.

Once the electrons were pulled into atoms, the light was no longer trapped in a fog of particles. This is when the universe emitted its first light! To see how this early light left us a big clue, turn to page 20!

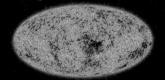

⋆Astrotales

The Father of the Big Bang

Georges Lemaitre
1884–1966

The "father" of the Big Bang idea was actually *really* a Father! His name was Georges Lemaitre, and he was a Belgian Catholic priest and cosmologist. In 1931, he published a scientific paper describing the idea that the universe began with the explosion of a single tiny particle at a single point in time. The universe has been expanding, Lemaitre explained, ever since.

Edwin Hubble's observations backed up the idea of the expanding universe (see below), and soon the idea took hold, causing a huge revolution in science.

Nowadays, most cosmologists don't say that the Big Bang erupted from a single *particle*. Since we have no observations or experimental data to back this up, we can't say scientifically what the pre-universe looked like at (or *before*) its big birthday moment. All we can really say is that our universe started off much smaller and much hotter than it is now!

About a billion years   13.7 billion years

Stars and Galaxies Form

Finally, after hundreds of millions of years, gravity pulled gases together into the first galaxies, and the first stars began to shine.

The Present Era

Today, as the universe continues to expand, distant galaxies rush farther and farther away from ours. Astronomer Edwin Hubble first observed this in the 1920s, providing the first evidence to support the Big Bang theory. See pages 16–17 to find out more about this!

Edwin Hubble, 1889–1953

So, cadet, now you're ready to start examining all the clues in the Big Bang puzzle! As your first step, turn the page to *shed some light* on the kind of evidence that's headed your way....

So, how do we know how the universe began if it happened so long ago? Well, there are plenty of clues out there—and almost all of them are in the form of LIGHT WAVES.

Wondering how light holds clues to the story of the universe? Then say hello to master detective Hugh Niverse—he'll light the way for you!

> Stick with me, cadet, and you'll see the light!

Meet Detective Hugh Niverse

Hi, cadet, I'm detective Hugh Niverse, and I've been on the Big Bang case since it first opened more than seventy years ago. Time sure flies when you're solving the greatest puzzle of all time!

If you want to get clues to *any* of the puzzles of the universe, you have to really know your light waves—all the different kinds. That's my specialty! Cosmic detectives like me look out into the universe in all directions and gather as many different kinds of light as we can with our telescopes. Then we study the light to find clues. I'll show you the tricks of the trade on the next few pages!

MAKING WAVES

To better understand how light waves work, let's consider another kind of wave: *sound* waves.

If you can hear something right now, then there are sound waves entering your ears. Say AHHH and touch your throat. Feel those vocal cords vibrate to make sound waves?

Just like vibrating vocal cords make sound waves, vibrating atoms produce light waves. The kind of **light that's produced depends on how fast the atom shakes.**

Atoms with lots of energy produce light with *shorter* wavelengths.

Atoms with *less* energy produce light with *longer* waveleng

Try the mission on the next page to make some waves of your own!

SHAKE IT UP!

Light comes in lots of different varieties—there's visible light in every color of the rainbow, and then there's all the light we *can't* see, like X rays and radio waves. So what's the big difference? It's all about *wavelength*, as you'll see in this mission!

Launch Objective

▷ **Make waves!**

Your equipment

▶ **Metal spring** SPACE Case

Personnel

▶ **A friend**

Mission Procedure

1 You and your friend each take one end of the spring and stand about 5 feet (1.5 m) apart. Each of you should hold at least five coils.

2 Have your friend hold the spring still while you move your end up and down *slowly*. What is the *wavelength* of the waves you make: big or small?

3 Now speed up! Move your hand up and down really fast and watch what happens to the wavelength of your waves. Does it increase or decrease?

4 **More Wave Action:** If you move your hand higher up and lower down while you shake the spring, you'll create waves with greater height, or *amplitude*. The amplitude of a wave determines how bright the light is (or in the case of sound waves, how *loud* the sound is).

Science, Please!

As you saw in this mission, when you shake the spring fast, you get shorter wavelengths, and when you shake the spring slower, you get longer wavelengths. In the same way, when atoms vibrate, they produce shorter waves when they shake fast (when they have a lot of energy), and longer waves when they shake slower (when they have less energy). This results in all the different kinds of light you see below!

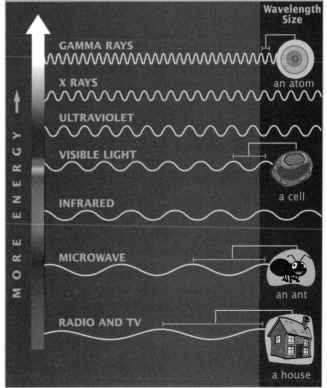

Wavelength Size

GAMMA RAYS — an atom

X RAYS

ULTRAVIOLET

VISIBLE LIGHT — a cell

INFRARED

MICROWAVE — an ant

RADIO AND TV — a house

MORE ENERGY

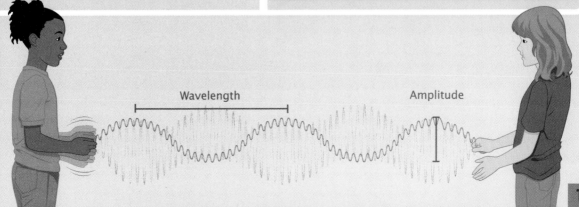

Wavelength

Amplitude

The ULTIMATE Speed Limit

N ow that you've investigated all the different kinds of light, there's one important thing to know about *all* of them—they're very *FAST*.

CATCH ME IF YOU CAN

As you might remember from your first month at Space U, light waves are the original speed demons. Nothing in the universe can ever catch up with them! How fast can they go? Well, stand up and jump right *now*. In the time it took you to jump and land, light would have zoomed all the way to the Moon! That's 186,000 miles (300,000 km) per *second*!

Light can reach the Moon in one and a half seconds!

Now, that's pretty fast for us here on our small planet, but space is a super huge place, so light has a long way to travel to get from place to place. It can take millions or even *billions* of years for light from a distant star or galaxy to speed through space and finally reach our eyes or telescopes.

COSMIC
SPEED LIMIT

186,000 miles
(300,000 km)

per second!

BACK IN TIME

So what does this light speed limit mean when you're looking for clues in places far off in space? It means that the farther away something is from us in space, the longer it takes for its light to reach us. So we're seeing things the way they *were* when light left them, not the way they are *now*. Try the next mission to see how you can peek billions of years into the past!

Light on Low Speed!

I f you could slow light down to the point that it crept along at 3 feet (1 m) per week, you'd be able to see into the past right in your own backyard!

Just imagine it: If you stood at one edge of your yard during the springtime, the far edge of the yard would look to you like it was back in winter! Why? Because you can only see things when light waves bounce off them and reach your eyes—and those waves would take *weeks* upon *weeks* to reach you! Think how weird it would be to hang out in your yard under *those* conditions!

OUT IN SPACE, BACK IN TIME

> Light takes so long to travel across the universe that looking out into space is like looking back in time. The farther out you look, the farther back you're seeing! What does that mean? Try this mission and see!

Launch Objective

> **Line up some Team Universe players and learn how long it takes their light to reach us!**

Your equipment

▶ **The following Team Universe cards: Blue Star, Cosmic Microwave Background Radiation, Earth, Moon, Pluto, Quasar, Spiral Galaxy, Star Cluster, and Sun**

Personnel

▶ **A friend to check your work**

Mission Procedure

1 Lay out the following Team Universe cards on a table or the floor:

 Home sweet home!

 Earth's night light.

 This is the spiral Whirlpool Galaxy.

 This blue star is Sirius, the brightest star in the sky. It's in the constellation Canis Major, the big dog.

 This little ball of rock and ice hangs out in the far reaches of our solar system.

 This is one of our galaxy's many star clusters.

 This is the oldest light in the universe!

 These are the bright cores of faraway galaxies. Even though they're far away, we can still see them because they're so bright.

 Your neighborhood star!

2 Place the Earth card in front of you.

3 Take the rest of the cards and lay them down in order of distance from the Earth, with the closest object being nearest to the Earth card, and the farthest object being—you guessed it—farthest.

4 On the next page (don't peek!) is the correct order of the cards. Have a friend check if your cards are in the right order. If there is any card that isn't in the right spot, have your friend tell you how many cards you got right before you made a mistake.

5 Keep trying until you get all the cards in the right order. Then turn the page to see how long it takes light from each of these objects to reach us!

Here's the correct order of the cards. What was going on here on Earth when the light from each of these objects started heading our way?

Cosmic Microwave Background

Time light takes to get here: 13.7 billion years

What was happening on Earth? Earth? There was no Earth! The universe was only 380,000 years old when this light was first emitted. See pages 20–21 to find out more about this!

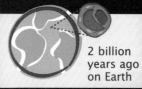

2 billion years ago on Earth

Quasar (3C273)

Time light takes to get here: 2 billion years

What was happening on Earth? The first cells were formed in the oceans.

37 million years ago on Earth

Spiral Galaxy (Whirlpool)

Time light takes to get here: 37 million years

What was happening on Earth? Mammals like elephants, rhinos, horses, dogs, and monkeys were around—but not *humans*!

4,600 years ago on Earth

Star Cluster (M37)

Time light takes to get here: 4,600 years

What was happening on Earth? Humans had invented the wheel, but not the alphabet!

8.6 years ago on Earth

Blue Star (Sirius)

Time light takes to get here: 8.6 years

What was happening on Earth? How old were you?

5.5 hours ago on Earth

Pluto

Time light takes to get here: 5.5 hours

What was happening on Earth? What were you doing?

8 minutes ago on Earth

Sun

Time light takes to get here: 8 minutes

What was happening on Earth? Maybe you were a few pages back?

Moon

Time light takes to get here: 1.5 seconds

What was happening on Earth? You were reading this sentence.

Science, Please!

The farther away something is from us in the universe, the longer it takes for the light to travel through space and reach our eyes (or our telescopes). This means that the deeper we look out into space, the farther back we're looking in time! We can never see the universe as it looks right now—we can only see how it looked in the past.

Let's think about this another way that's even more surprising. If there were another planet about 200 million light years away from us, and there were aliens on it right now with a super-amazing telescope that could see the surface of the Earth, would they see us? No! They'd see something much stranger—dinosaurs!

YIKES! Check out these alien monsters!

That's right, the light reaching the aliens right now from our planet would be 200 million years old, and that was when dinosaurs roamed the Earth. Quite a view!

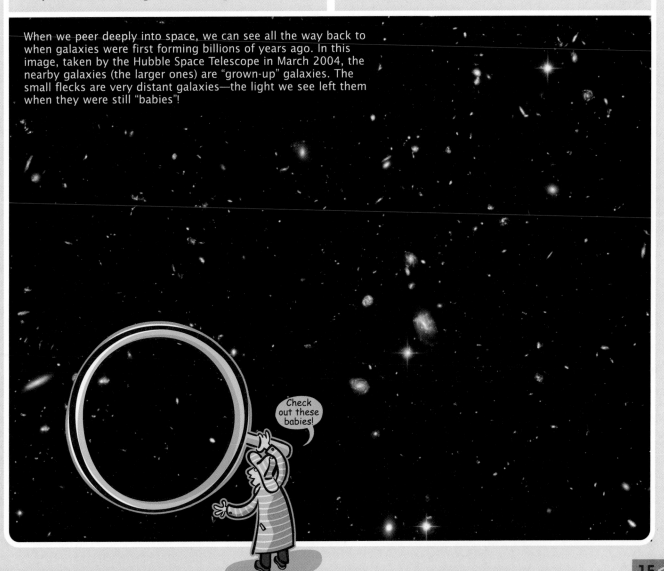

When we peer deeply into space, we can see all the way back to when galaxies were first forming billions of years ago. In this image, taken by the Hubble Space Telescope in March 2004, the nearby galaxies (the larger ones) are "grown-up" galaxies. The small flecks are very distant galaxies—the light we see left them when they were still "babies"!

Check out these babies!

Okay, cadet, now that we've got the basics squared away, it's time to open up the files and check out the evidence in the Big Bang case!

Edwin Hubble (1889-1953)

The first clue in the Big Bang case came from astronomer Edwin Hubble back in 1929.

Before Hubble came along, people thought that our Milky Way Galaxy was the entire universe. Hubble was the first to see that certain small cloudy-looking shapes in the night sky were actually other *galaxies*, meaning that our galaxy was just one of many in the universe!

But Hubble proved a lot more than that!

First, by studying a special kind of star in these distant galaxies, Hubble could determine how far away each galaxy was. These special stars, called Cepheid (SEFF-ee-id) Variables, get brighter and dimmer on a repeating cycle. Hubble knew how to use these stars as "cosmic mileposts," thanks to the clever detective work of another astronomer, Henrietta Leavitt.

Leave It to Leavitt

In 1912, Leavitt figured out a cool secret of Cepheid Variable stars: They get brighter and dimmer at a special speed that depends on their *absolute magnitude* (their actual brightness). A star's absolute magnitude is how bright it would be if it were exactly 32.6 light years away from us (that's a standard distance astronomers use to compare stars, since a very bright star will look dimmer to us if it's really far away, and a dim star will look brighter if it's closer).

Henrietta Leavitt (1868-1921)

Cepheid Variable star looking dim...

...and looking bright

Here's the galaxy M100 and one of its Cepheid Variable stars.

By timing how long a faraway Cepheid Variable took to go from its dimmest to its brightest, Leavitt could determine exactly how bright that star really was!

Hubble used Leavitt's stellar technique to find out the actual brightness of Cepheid Variable stars in distant galaxies. Then he compared that *actual* brightness to how bright the star looked when seen from Earth. And since we can calculate exactly how much a star's brightness will fade over distance, Hubble could determine how far away that star was, and therefore how far that star's *galaxy* was!

A Big Shift!

But then came the real shocker: Hubble discovered that light waves from these distant galaxies had stretched out—he called this *redshift* (see the Quick Blast below). The farther the galaxy, the more its light had stretched out. Hubble realized that all this stretching meant that...drum roll, please...

...the universe was expanding in all directions like an inflating balloon!

Whoa! Suddenly it looked very different out there. No longer was the universe small and unchanging—it was getting bigger and bigger every moment! To expand *your* understanding of these big ideas, try the Quick Blast below and the mission on the next page!

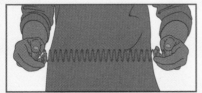

Seeing Redshift

Hubble used *redshift* to figure out that the universe was expanding. What does it mean when light waves are redshifted? Grab your metal spring from your Space Case and get *reddy* to find out!

1 Hold one end of the spring in each hand. Stretch the spring out and look at the "light wave" that forms.

2 Now move your hands farther apart. Do you see how the coils of the spring stretch out? It's the

same with light waves out in space. As the universe expands, the light waves that are moving through it get stretched out, too!

3 Why is this effect called "redshift"? It's because red is the visible color with the most stretched-out waves (or the longest *wavelengths*), as you can see below. So, when light waves get more stretched out, they look redder! (And when light waves get more smushed together, they look bluer, and we call them "blueshifted"!)

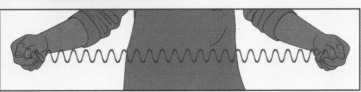

BALLOON

We know that the universe is expanding because we can see that distant galaxies are all moving away from our own. In this mission, you'll make a model of the expanding universe and observe how distant galaxies make their getaways!

Launch Objective

> Blow up your own mini-universe and explore expansion!

Your equipment

▶ Balloon **Space Case**
▶ Glow-in-the-dark stickers **Space Case**
▶ Lamp
▶ Dark room
▶ Mirror
▶ Small removable sticky note (optional)
▶ String
▶ Red and blue markers
▶ Ruler

Personnel

▶ A friend to help measure

Mission Procedure

Part 1: Expansion in Action

1 Start by blowing up your balloon partway. Hold the balloon shut and place your stickers in an even pattern on its surface. The stickers stand for galaxies, and the black balloon is the space between them.

2 Hold your partially blown-up balloon under a lamp for a few minutes to activate the glow-in-the-dark galaxies. Then let the air out of the balloon and prepare for your expansion extravaganza!

3 Now go into a dark room and stand in front of a mirror. Blow up the

balloon (not too much, we don't want this universe to burst!) and watch the expansion in the mirror. As the balloon expands, it carries the dots with it, moving them farther and farther apart, just like the expanding universe carries galaxies with it!

Part 2: Go the Distance

1 Turn the lights back on and let some of the air out of the balloon until it's about the size of your outstretched hand. Have your friend hold the balloon closed so you can do the next step.

2 Pick out one dot to be your home galaxy. Mark it by placing a small sticky note near the dot or by coloring the dot with one of your markers.

Home galaxy

3 Pick two more dots— one *near* your home galaxy, and another *far away*. Then carefully remove all the other dots except those two and your home galaxy.

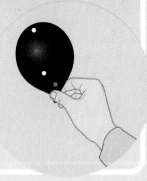

4 Place one end of your string on your home galaxy. Run the string along the balloon to your nearby galaxy and make a mark on the string where that galaxy is located, using your blue marker.

5 Then measure from your home galaxy to your faraway galaxy and mark the string with the *red* marker.

6 Now blow your balloon up so it's bigger and have your friend hold it shut for you again. Lay the string on the balloon with one end on your home galaxy and mark the new location of the nearby galaxy using the blue marker. Do the same for the faraway galaxy, using the red marker.

7 Congrats, cadet! You have now collected your galactic data! Now lay the string along your ruler and measure the distance between the two blue marks.

8 Repeat step 7 for the two red marks.

9 Compare the distance that each galaxy moved. What do you discover?

Science, Please!

Just like in the real universe, as your balloon universe expands, it carries the glowing galaxies along for the ride. The galaxies *themselves* don't get any bigger as the universe stretches out, but the space between them grows and grows.

When you measured the distances covered by the nearby and faraway galaxies, you should have found that the faraway galaxy covered a greater distance than the nearby one did. That's because there's a lot more space (or balloon) between your home galaxy and the faraway one. As the balloon's surface stretched out, all that space expanded between your home galaxy and your distant neighbor galaxy. There was much *less* space to expand between your galaxy and your nearby neighbor.

So, because there's more space-stretching, the *light waves* coming to us from the distant galaxy get stretched out (or "redshifted") a lot more than the light waves from the nearer galaxy. That's exactly what Edwin Hubble observed in 1929 (back up to page 16 for the full story!). This was the big clue that led him to the discovery that the universe was expanding!

Cosmic Crash!

But wait! There's one more thing you need to know to get the whole picture. Even though your balloon showed *all* galaxies moving away from each other, that's not exactly what happens in the real universe.

In the real universe, galaxies are grouped together in clusters. The galaxy *clusters* move apart from each other as the universe expands, but galaxies within the same cluster can actually be moving *closer* to each other—and some can even collide! Why? One word: gravity! Galaxies have very strong gravity, and when they're close enough to each other, their gravity draws them closer together, overpowering the effects of expansion.

So, after Edwin Hubble's big breakthrough, cosmic detectives knew that the universe was growing larger. But how could they find out what the universe's early moments were like?

First Light

If the baby universe was really hot and bright, like the Big Bang theory says, then we should still be able to detect that early light (since looking out into space is looking back in time). This high-energy light would have stretched out as the universe expanded, so the light would now have much longer wavelengths—it would be in the form of *microwave radiation*.

Microwave radiation has long wavelengths.

A Strange Hiss

So, does this microwave radiation exist? Sure does! First detected in 1965, the "cosmic microwave background," or CMB, covers the sky. It's everywhere in the universe, providing good evidence for the Big Bang theory.

We can't see this microwave radiation with our eyes, but we can detect it with radio telescopes (which pick up wavelengths in the microwave and radio range). The CMB is like a faint "hiss" that radio telescopes detect everywhere they're pointed. In fact, the astronomers who discovered the CMB thought at first that something was wrong with their equipment! They even kicked out the pigeons that had nested inside their giant telescope, thinking *they* were causing the hiss!

It wasn't me!

The two radio astronomers who first detected the CMB, Robert Wilson and Arno Penzias, stand in front of their horn-shaped radio telescope. They were awarded the Nobel Prize in 1978 for their discovery!

Microwave Map

In 2003, this very detailed map was created of the CMB. With this map, scientists could determine the exact age of the universe—13.7 billion years—and see the earliest seeds of today's galaxy clusters!

This map shows the microwave radiation in our sky, the faint glow of the universe's earliest light, emitted 380,000 years after the Big Bang. The map is oval-shaped because it's our sky projected onto a flat surface—you've probably seen maps of Earth that are oval-shaped, and this is the same idea.

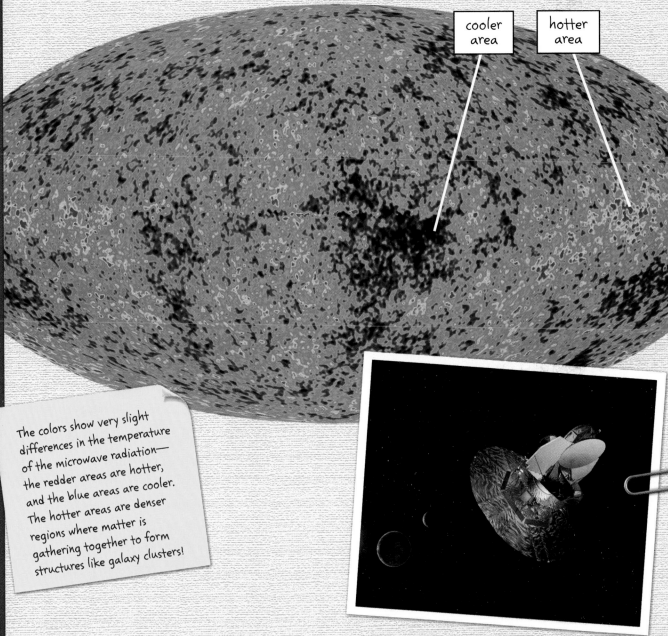

cooler area

hotter area

The colors show very slight differences in the temperature of the microwave radiation—the redder areas are hotter, and the blue areas are cooler. The hotter areas are denser regions where matter is gathering together to form structures like galaxy clusters!

The map was created with data from this satellite, called WMAP.

Another great clue in the Big Bang case has to do with helium—the stuff you find inside birthday balloons!

Building Blocks

The first ingredients in the early universe were particles like protons and neutrons, the building blocks of all the elements.

The simplest element—with only a single proton—is hydrogen. There are more hydrogen atoms in the universe than any other kind.

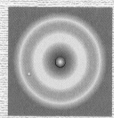

Hydrogen atom

To make bigger atoms like helium, protons and neutrons have to be forced to fuse or stick together. It takes a LOT of energy and VERY high temperatures to do that. Nowadays, only stars are hot enough to make helium fusion happen!

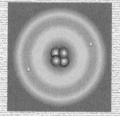

Helium atom

But if the universe had once been really small and hot, then helium could have been made back then. That means we'd see much more helium in our universe than if stars alone were making it. That's a cool (or not so cool!) way to see if the Big Bang theory checks out!

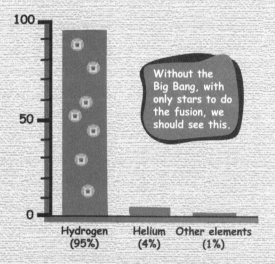

Without the Big Bang, with only stars to do the fusion, we should see this.

Hydrogen (95%) Helium (4%) Other elements (1%)

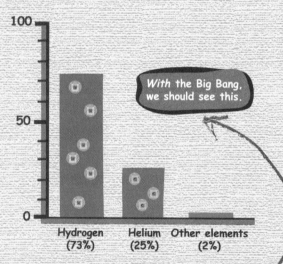

With the Big Bang, we should see this.

Hydrogen (73%) Helium (25%) Other elements (2%)

Now for the big moment: How much helium do we actually find when we look out into the universe?

We find the amount of helium predicted by the Big Bang theory!

What an exciting clue! Stars couldn't have made all the helium in the universe by themselves, so the Big Bang had to have helped!

LITTLE Bangs!

Scientists can also look for clues about the Big Bang by making little bangs!

A huge machine called a *particle accelerator* can take tiny particles like protons and rev them up really fast—close to the speed of light—and then BANG them together! This smashes the particles into even smaller bits, which scientists can analyze. It's kind of like studying the inner workings of a TV by dropping it off a skyscraper and looking at the shattered pieces!

These itty-bitty bangs are really helpful because all their energy recreates what the universe was like just after the Big Bang—and we can watch this time!

About 30 feet (9 m) underground, below the 4-mile (6.4-km) ring you see here, is a powerful particle accelerator called the Tevatron, located at a laboratory called Fermilab in Illinois. Inside the Tevatron, protons and particles called antiprotons fly around at 99.9999 percent of the speed of light. They're then smashed into each other so scientists can watch the pieces that fly out!

The particles that fly around the Tevatron start off as hydrogen atoms inside this underground machine, which begins the acceleration process.

The Tevatron's underground tunnel

Particles zoom through a tube that runs inside these giant magnets.

When particles smash into each other inside a detector, they leave behind tracks like these. If a particle has an electric charge, it twirls around in the magnetic field of the detector and creates a curly line. If the particle has no charge, it makes a straight line.

Well, cadet, it's time for you to *make tracks* to your next case! But *this* case is not closed by any means! As we build faster and faster particle accelerators, we can learn more and more about our universe's tiny building blocks—and about the Big Bang that made them. Hopefully we're on the *right track* to great new discoveries!

Part 2: The Case of Space and Time

Welcome to your next case, cadet! To begin, we'll ask a very basic question:

WHAT IS SPACE?

Just like you need a canvas or a piece of paper to paint a picture, the stuff in the universe needs to be painted on something, too—and the canvas is *space*. How is the universe like a painting?

- Instead of paint we have *matter*, which is made up of atoms.

- So what is the brush? Forces like gravity and magnetism pull and move matter, helping to paint the picture of the universe.

- Now the final question is: What is the canvas? We know it as "space," but what is space, really? How can we describe it?

HOW DO WE MEASURE SPACE?

One way to describe something is to measure it. Let's try to measure space by starting with your Space Case. Since it's a box, you need to measure its *length*, its *width*, and finally its *height*. These three measurements are the three *dimensions* of the box—they give you all the information you need to make another box the exact same size.

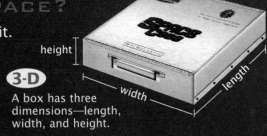

3-D
A box has three dimensions—length, width, and height.

We call any dimension that tells us about space a *spatial* dimension. You know the three you move around in as *left-right*, *up-down*, and *forward-backward*. But if you didn't have all of these directions available to you, what would life be like? Try the next mission to imagine life in a flat, 2-D world, where up and down no longer exist!

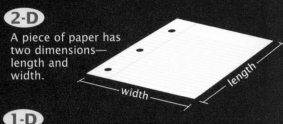

2-D
A piece of paper has two dimensions—length and width.

1-D
A line can be measured in just one direction—length.

ADVENTURES IN FLATLAND

Can you imagine what your life would be like if your world was two-dimensional —if you were squashed flat and stuck on a sheet of paper that you could move around on, but not get off? In this mission, you'll meet some characters who live in that kind of world. See what life is like for them!

Launch Objective

> **Learn about life in 2-D by creating Flatland.**

Your equipment

▶ Flatland Log pages
▶ Scissors

Mission Procedure

Part 1: Build Your 2-D Flatland

1 Print out the Flatland Log pages from the Space U web site (www.scholastic.com/space) and cut out each shape. Or, draw and cut out your own shapes like the ones pictured below.

2 Lay out all your shapes on a flat surface—this is your Flatland! Once your shapes are settled in Flatland, you can't pick them up again—they're stuck in the two dimensions of their space. They can only slide around—there's no up or down for them! This also means that nothing can overlap with anything else. Two things on top of each other would mean that there is an *up*—and that doesn't exist in Flatland!

House #1

House #2

Trish   Fred   Ralph   Slim   Ursula   Marge

Part 2: Explore Flatland!

Now that you've got Flatland set up, see if you can answer the questions below:

1 When Fred meets Ralph, what will they look like to each other? How would Trish look to Fred?

Ralph   Fred   Trish

2 Which character could be *either* the longest or the shortest?

3 Who can live in house #1?

4 Who can live in house #2?

5 Put Ursula and Fred next to each other. Then, break the rules of Flatland—lift Ursula up over Fred and put her down on his other side. What would this look like to Fred?

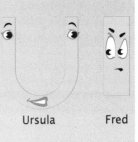
Ursula   Fred

6 What if *you* visited Flatland? What if Marge saw you—what would she tell the others about you?

Here's what happens in Flatland:

1 All of the characters in Flatland would see each other as only a line, since no one could move "up" above to see the shapes that you can see! To get an idea of how things look in Flatland, hold each character flat in front of you and look at its edge.

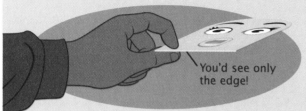

You'd see only the edge!

2 Slim could be very, very long or very, very short, depending on the angle someone saw him from.

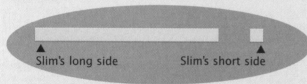

▲ Slim's long side   Slim's short side ▲

3 Nobody can get inside house #1! There's no door to enter through, and the characters couldn't hop over the walls without entering into the third dimension.

4 Fred or Slim can fit into house #2. No one else can fit through the door, but Ursula and Trish can visit—Ursula can stick one of her arms inside, and Trish can poke her head in.

5 Fred would see Ursula mysteriously vanish from one side of him when you picked her up, then reappear on his other side when you set her down.

6 The flat people could see only a slice of you at a time. So, as you stepped into their world, your footprints would make two new lines appear to them. If you got down on your hands and knees, they'd see lines made by your handprints, knee prints, and the tops of your feet. The inhabitants of Flatland wouldn't even know that the mysteriously appearing lines came from a single person!

So, now you know what it's like to miss out on a dimension! Is it possible that *we're* like the Flatlanders—could there be other spatial dimensions that *we* can't see or experience?

Yes, it *is* possible! According to some theories, there could be as many as *eleven* dimensions in our universe. Many of these dimensions, though, are thought to be very tiny (much smaller than atoms), invisible even to our most powerful magnifying devices!

And *here's* a surprise cadet—dimensions don't always have to be about space! We have another very important dimension in our universe—do you know what that might be? Check out the next page to find out!

THE MARRIAGE OF
SPACE AND TIME

So, cadet, you know the three dimensions we move around in, but did you know that you're *also* moving through *another* dimension right now as you read? That's right—and that dimension is...TIME!

The idea that time was a dimension came from Albert Einstein in 1905. His "Special Theory of Relativity" united space and time forever as *space-time*!

> I now pronounce you space-time!

HOW IS TIME A DIMENSION?

Think about it this way: Anytime something happens in the universe, it happens somewhere at a specific *time*. Just say you arrange to meet your friend at 465 First Avenue, 2nd Floor, at 3:30 p.m. Even if you make it to the right *place*, if you're there at a different *time*, you won't meet your friend!

Your meeting has to take place in *space* at a *time*, and Einstein called this an *event*.

So, thanks to Einstein, space and time were forever wedded to each other. From then on, time would be the fourth dimension!

But how did Einstein come to this discovery? And how did it change the way we understand time? Turn the page to find out!

Albert Einstein— a *relatively* famous mind! Get to know him on page 34!

Meet Detective Lotte DeMension

Hi, cadet, I'm detective Lotte DeMension—"Lotte" as in "lotta" fun! I'm going to be your guide through *The Case of Space and Time*. Mine is not an easy job, let me tell you. I'll be riding a train at almost light speed, flying a spacecraft out of the solar system, and hunting for black holes! But it's all for a good cause—introducing *you* to the marvels of space-time!

Albert Einstein was always asking big questions. As a child, he often imagined what would happen if he could chase after a beam of light *at light speed*. Would the light look like it was standing still?

This was a big problem to solve, and Einstein came up with a big idea: He thought that everyone in the universe, no matter how fast they were traveling, would always see light moving away from them at the same speed, the speed of light.

Can yo
light? R

This means that light behaves like no other moving thing we know. you why, Detective Lotte DeMension will board the Space U Express T her twin brother, Max, will stand beside the tracks to watch!

If Lotte throws a baseball at 50 miles per hour while the going 50 miles per hour, Max will see the ball moving at per hour (the train's speed plus the ball's speed).

If Lotte rides her motorcycle at 100 miles per hour corridor while the train is going 50 miles per hour, Lotte riding past at—you guessed it—150 miles pe

But if Lotte turns on a flashlight (and Ma: light-speed timer), will Max measure the traveling at light speed *plus* 50 miles per light will *still* be traveling at light speed! beam traveling at light speed, too!

Now let's speed up th
light speed (hang on,
turns on the flashligh
and Max each see it t
they'd both see it mo
then you're right up t

So, how can light speed be the same for everyone, no matte they're moving?

To figure out this brain-buster, think about what speed is:

DISTANCE	÷	TIME	=	SPEED
Travel 2 miles in		1 hour		= 2 miles per hour
Travel 4 miles in		2 hours		= 2 miles per hour

So, the two things to consider here are **distance** and **time**. Look back at the final situation on the previous page. Did both Max and Lotte see the light travel the same distance?

From Max's Point of View

■ Max would have seen the light beam travel a much greater distance than Lotte did, because the train was whizzing by him so fast.

From Lotte's Point of View

■ Inside the train, Lotte would have seen the light beam travel just the length of the train car. Since she's moving with the train, she sees the same thing she would see if the train were still.

So, Lotte and Max don't see the light travel the same distance. In order for them to both see light traveling at the same *speed*, then there also have to be differences in the way they're experiencing *time*.

And that's where the cool part comes in: From Max's point of view, Lotte is actually moving through time *slower* than he is! In fact, the faster Lotte moves through space, the slower she will move through time compared to Max! That's the amazing thing that Einstein realized: The faster we move through space, the slower we move through time!

You might be thinking: Wait a minute, I've never seen time go any slower for someone who's moving faster than I am. And you're right—we don't normally see any differences in the way we move through time because we don't usually travel very fast. But if we could move at almost the speed of light, we'd see this effect happen *big time*!

In fact, if Lotte hopped into her spacecraft and sped off into space at *almost* light speed and returned three weeks later (according to *her* calendar), she'd find that her twin, Max, was forty years older! Whoa!

Lotte would have seen her watch ticking away normally during her three-week trip, and Max would have seen his watch ticking normally, too, for the forty years of his life that passed while Lotte was gone. But when Lotte returned, they'd see that Lotte's experience of time had been very different from Max's!

If you want to see some proof of these brain-bending ideas, just turn the page!

The amazing ideas you learned about on the previous pages come from Einstein's Special Theory of Relativity. It's called "relativity" because it says that your observations of space and time are always *relative* to you (they're from *your* frame of reference)—they're not the same for everyone.

It's hard to believe that things can really move through time at different rates. Want proof? Here you go!

Long Live the Muons

Muons are particles that are created when high-energy gamma rays from space hit the atoms in our atmosphere, breaking the atoms up into particles. These muons live a very, very short time—only a micro-second—before they die in a puff of energy.

So, when we were able to start detecting muons down here on Earth's surface, it was a big mystery. How did they live long enough to make it all the way down here to us?

Einstein's theory solved the mystery: The muons were moving so fast—almost the speed of light—that to us they appeared to live much longer than a micro-second! But to the muons, life was still just a micro-second long!

QuickBlast

Plane Old Time!

Muons can travel at nearly the speed of light. But what about things that *don't* move that fast—can we see any difference at all in the way they move through time?

In one experiment, two very precise clocks were set together. One clock was put on an airplane and taken for a long, fast ride. The other clock, meanwhile, sat on the ground. When the plane landed, its clock was:

A) Still showing the same time as the one on the ground.

B) A tiny fraction of a second *ahead* of the one on the ground.

C) A tiny fraction of a second *behind* the one on the ground.

What do you think happened? Use what you know about relativity to make a prediction, and then turn to page 48 to see how the experiment turned out!

The FABRIC of Space-Time

Always asking questions, Einstein had another big curiosity after he finished his Special Theory of Relativity. And that was: How does gravity work? How does it reach out across space from a star to a planet, or from a planet to a moon? What *carries* gravity?

And with his General Theory of Relativity, he found the answer. Einstein gave us a new view of the universe in which space-time was a fabric that could be warped by stars, planets, and anything else with mass. The more mass, the bigger the warp.

Things that get close to these warps will be pulled into them (right now, for example, you're being pulled into Earth's warp!). And that's how gravity works, by warping the fabric of the cosmos!

Turn the page to start exploring the wonders of space-time warps!

We all have mass and warp space-time, but our warps are so small that nothing falls into them!

SPACE-TIME WARP!

The fabric of space-time bends and warps around planets, stars, and other massive objects. Want to create your own warps and watch things fall into them and orbit around them? Then grab your space-time fabric and let's get rolling!

Launch Objective

▶ **Warp space-time!**

Your equipment

▶ **Large, sturdy cardboard box at least 12 inches (30 cm) on its shortest side (an office paper box works well)**
▶ **Ruler, yardstick, or meterstick**
▶ **Pencil**
▶ **Tape**
▶ **Space-time fabric grid** SPACE Case
▶ **Stapler**
▶ **Two or more binder clips or clothespins**
▶ **Two balls** SPACE Case

Personnel

▶ **An Intergalactic Adult (IGA) to help with stapling**

Mission Procedure

Part 1: Set Up Your Grid

1 First, you need to make a square frame for your space-time fabric. To prepare your cardboard box, fold all its flaps down into the box so they won't be in your way.

2 Measure the short side of your box. Then lay your ruler along the top of each long side of the box and make a mark the same distance as the length of your box's short side.

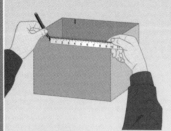

3 Lay your ruler across the box from one mark to the other and tape it firmly in place. If your ruler is not long enough, use a yardstick or meterstick instead.

4 Lay your space-time fabric over the top of your square frame and stretch it tight.

5 Have your IGA open up a stapler to staple the fabric to the box on the three cardboard sides. On the fourth side, where your ruler is, fold the fabric over the ruler and hold it in place with binder clips or clothespins. Your space-time grid is ready!

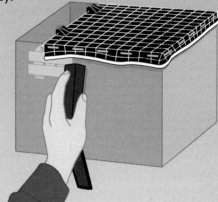

Part 2: That's Really Warped!

Now that you've set up your grid, try these warped situations!

Situation 1: Place the large ball in the center of the space-time fabric by itself. Now take the small ball, put it anywhere on the fabric, and just let it go. What happens?

Situation 2: Now put one finger on the big ball in the center and gently press on it. What happens to the grid as you push on the ball? While pressing the ball down, again place the little ball in different places around the grid and let it go. What happens this time?

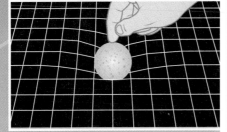

Situation 3: Still pressing down on the big ball in the center, hold the small ball near the edge of your fabric. Give the small ball a little push to send it around the big one in a circle, or orbit. Keep trying until you get a good orbit. What happens to the orbit over time?

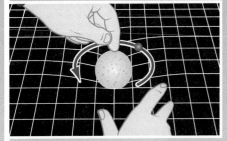

Science, Please!

Let's see what was going on with your space-time fabric, looking at your three situations:

Situation 1: When you dropped your small ball, it should have fallen into the warp created by the larger ball. This is exactly what happens when something falls toward the Earth. You can experience this yourself right now—just jump up, and you'll fall back down to the Earth. You're inside Earth's warp, and you're always being pulled down into it!

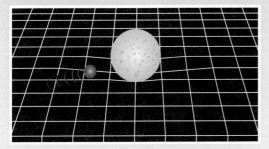

Situation 2: When you pressed down on the big ball, you made it act like a heavier ball (a ball with more mass). You should have seen the warp grow deeper as you pressed harder on the ball. When you released the little ball, it should have fallen into the warp faster than it did before.

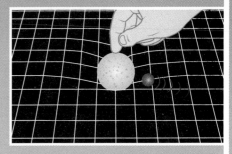

In real space-time, massive planets like Jupiter create bigger warps (and therefore have more gravity) than less massive planets like Earth. The bigger the warp, the stronger the pull of gravity, and the faster objects will fall into the warp.

Situation 3: Orbits happen when a smaller mass goes around a larger mass at just the right speed—not too slow (in which case it would fall into the warp), and not too fast (in which case it would fly past the warp).

You probably found you could make the small ball go around the warp a few times before it spiraled down and dropped into the warp. The ball finally falls in because it rubs on the fabric and slows down due to *friction*. If there were no friction, your small ball could keep circling forever, even with the warp trying to pull it down! That's why planets keep orbiting the Sun, and why moons keep orbiting planets—they don't have friction out in space to slow them down.

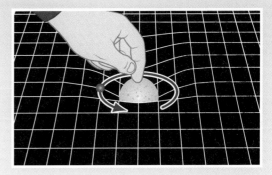

Your space-time fabric grid gave you a good view of one *slice* of space-time, but real space-time is not just a two-dimensional sheet. The warping happens in all spatial dimensions! Imagine a warp not only below the ball, but also above it and on its sides, and you'll get the idea!

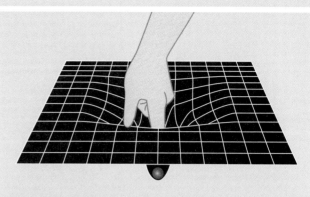

More from Mission Control

Want to try to make a *really* deep warp in space-time? Then try pressing really hard on the small ball to simulate a lot of mass packed into a small space, like a neutron star (a dense ball of neutrons left behind after a massive star dies). You might also look around for other balls that are naturally heavier. See how deep you can make your warps!

And when you're ready to check out the *ultimate* space-time warp, head over to page 36!

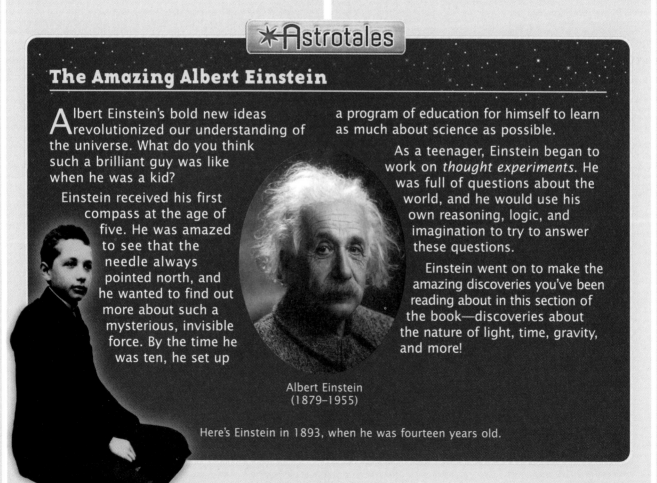

✶Astrotales

The Amazing Albert Einstein

Albert Einstein's bold new ideas revolutionized our understanding of the universe. What do you think such a brilliant guy was like when he was a kid?

Einstein received his first compass at the age of five. He was amazed to see that the needle always pointed north, and he wanted to find out more about such a mysterious, invisible force. By the time he was ten, he set up a program of education for himself to learn as much about science as possible.

As a teenager, Einstein began to work on *thought experiments*. He was full of questions about the world, and he would use his own reasoning, logic, and imagination to try to answer these questions.

Einstein went on to make the amazing discoveries you've been reading about in this section of the book—discoveries about the nature of light, time, gravity, and more!

Albert Einstein
(1879–1955)

Here's Einstein in 1893, when he was fourteen years old.

How can we see proof of Einstein's idea that mass creates warps in space-time? Well, we know that objects that pass by warps are affected by them—their paths *curve* around the warps, as you saw in the last mission.

Einstein knew that light from stars should curve around warps, too. And what better way to observe this than by looking at how starlight bends around the warp created by our Sun!

But there's one problem: The Sun is so bright that we can't see the stars that are near it in the sky. So, how can we block out the Sun? Fortunately, that's exactly what the Moon does during a solar eclipse!

Sun Block

So, in 1919, a team of astronomers led by Sir Arthur Eddington went to the island of Principe, off the coast of West Africa, to watch a solar eclipse. During the brief moment when the Moon hid the Sun, they were able to see the stars around the Sun in the sky—and these stars were not *exactly* where the star charts said they'd be!

The star looks like it's here

But *really* the star is here!

The Sun's warp in space-time bends the path of starlight!

How could these stars have moved? They didn't! Their light just got bent by the Sun's warp, which made the stars *look* like they were in different places! This clue was *stellar* evidence to prove Einstein's theory:

Mass *does* warp space-time!

This was front-page news in 1919, and it changed science forever!

LIGHTS ALL ASKEW IN THE HEAVENS

Men of Science More or Less Agog Over Results of Eclipse Observations.

EINSTEIN THEORY TRIUMPHS

Stars Not Where They Seemed or Were Calculated to be, but Nobody Need Worry.

A BOOK FOR 12 WISE MEN

No More in All the World Could Comprehend It, Said Einstein When His Daring Publishers Accepted It.

Special Cable to THE NEW YORK TIMES.
LONDON, Nov. 9.—Efforts made to put in words intelligible to the non-scientific public the Einstein theory of light proved by the eclipse expedition so far have not been very successful. The new theory was discussed at a recent meeting of the Royal Society and Royal Astronomical Society, Sir Joseph Thomson, President of the Royal Society, declares it is not possible to put Einstein's theory into really intelligible words, at the same time Thomson adds:
"The results of the eclipse expedi

The Ultimate Warp!

So, cadet, are you ready to experience the *ultimate* space-time warp? If you've completed **Mission: Space-Time Warp** on pages 32–34 (back up if you haven't!), then you know that a very massive object creates a *really* deep warp in the fabric of space-time.

What do you think an *infinitely* massive object would do to space-time? Could it rip a hole in the fabric of the universe? If that seems too weird and wild to be true, then welcome to the world of...

BLACK HOLES!

A black hole has so much mass squeezed into such a tiny area that the fabric of space-time is no longer able to hold it all up. The warp is so deep—*infinitely* deep—that you could say it tears a hole in the fabric of space-time.

Event Horizon

The size of a black hole is measured by its outer edge, called the *event horizon*. This edge is the point of no return for anything falling toward the black hole. If you, your favorite superhero, or even *light* goes past the event horizon, there's no coming back out!

CHOOSE YOUR SIZE

Black holes come in many different sizes:

1) Event horizons are as small as an atom.

1) The smallest black holes, called *primordial black holes*, can be the size of an atom and have the same mass as an entire mountain! They were created by the Big Bang, and there are very few, if any, left in the universe. (*Primordial* means "existing from the very beginning.")

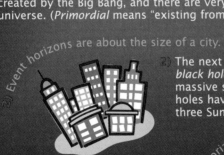

2) Event horizons are about the size of a city.

2) The next size up are the *stellar black holes*, left over after the most massive stars die. These black holes have the mass of at least three Suns.

3) Event horizons are about the size of planet Earth.

3) Then there are even bigger black holes, called *intermediate-mass black holes*, that have 100 to 1,000 times the mass of our Sun.

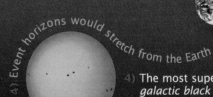

4) Event horizons would stretch from the Earth to the Sun!

4) The most super of them all are the *galactic black holes*, found in the center of many (or maybe even most!) galaxies, including our own Milky Way. These monsters have as much mass as millions of Suns!

On the next few pages, we're going to hunt for a stellar black hole, then send a robot inside to explore it. Get ready for a really *warped* adventure!

FIND a Black Hole!

If we want to visit a black hole, we need to find one first. But how can we see something that gives off no light?

LURKING IN THE DARK

If a black hole is all by itself out there in space, then we might *never* see it! You'd only know you were near one if you got close enough to feel a tug from its gravity. But don't worry, cadet, here in our solar system we're safe!

X MARKS THE SPOT

Astronomers discover black holes when stars or nebulae come near enough to the hole that some of their gas falls toward it. As the gas swirls into the black hole, it forms a whirling disk called an *accretion disk*.

Inside this cosmic tornado, the gas gets very, very hot as its atoms speed up. This hot gas gives off lots of energy in the form of X-ray radiation. So astronomers find black hole "suspects" in space by looking for X-ray clues!

Now that you know what to look for, turn the page to find a black hole and start exploring!

✳Astrotales

Black Hole Eats Star!

In 2003, NASA's Chandra X-Ray Observatory telescope witnessed for the first time what happens when a star gets too close to a black hole.

Scientists watched in suspense as a distant star bumped another star into the path of a super-massive black hole. The star was pulled toward the black hole, stretching out as it got nearer and nearer. Then, the black hole's gravity ripped the star apart and threw its gas back out into the galaxy—but not without swallowing some of the star, too!

The black hole only ate about 1 percent of the star, but even this small gulp released a huge amount of energy—like the amount that's released when a massive star explodes in a supernova! Why so much energy? It's because the gas was whirling so incredibly fast right before it passed the event horizon and fell into the black hole

WATCH THE ACTION!

Space U cadets can watch a black hole chow down on a star at www.scholastic.com/space!

Take the Black Hole Plunge!

Ever wonder what would happen if you fell into a black hole? Well, Detective Lotte DeMension and her robot, Sparky, are just about to answer that question for you! Well, *Sparky* will answer it, anyway—and Lotte will watch!

PREP FOR THE JOURNEY

To start the expedition, Lotte finds a nice stellar-mass black hole and parks her spacecraft a good distance away from it. She preps Sparky for the journey, giving him a flashlight and instructing him to flash it once per second. Lotte will also flash her own light once per second. That way, each one will be able to see how quickly time is passing for the other. Also, we'll be able to see how light waves are affected by the black hole. Once the prep work is complete, brave Sparky starts to head toward the black hole. To find out what happens, read the journals below!

Lotte's Journal

As Sparky nears the event horizon, I see the light coming from his flashlight start to get redder as it loses energy. His flashes also get slower and slower—the black hole's strong gravity makes him appear to move through time more slowly!

Soon, Sparky's light seems to fade out, but I quickly switch on my infrared camera and see that his light is now in the infrared range. His flashes are getting slower...and slower...to the point that they seem to have stopped.

My last view is of Sparky hovering over the event horizon, frozen in time. Then he blinks out, because the light coming from Sparky is now in the form of radio waves. I never see him fall in!

Sparky's Journal

Things are pretty smooth for me until I get close to the event horizon. Then I look back at Lotte, and I see that her flashes are getting faster and faster. Her flashlight also starts to look bluer and bluer because its light is gaining energy as it falls into the black hole. The light continues to gain energy until it blinks out, becoming ultraviolet, then X-ray, then gamma-ray light!

Then...whoa! I start to feel a strong pull on my feet. Soon, my whole body gets stretched out like a piece of spaghetti! And then I.................

Well, unfortunately, there is no more Sparky at this point. A split second after he stretched out, he was ripped apart and all the atoms that made him up fell into the center of the black hole. Yikes!

So, without a doubt, as Sparky can attest, black holes are *not* safe for travel! But are there other holes in the universe that *might* be? Check out the next page!

What if there are hidden "shortcuts" in space-time that we could use to travel to a distant place or time? It sounds like science-fiction, but it *is* possible that such "shortcuts" could exist, and we call them...

WORM HOLES!

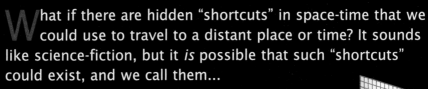

To imagine a worm hole, think of our universe as a piece of paper. Two points might be far from each other on the paper, but if you fold the paper, you could connect the two points with a tube. That's a worm hole!

But could we ever really *use* a worm hole? A lot of problems would have to be overcome first. For example, according to current theories:

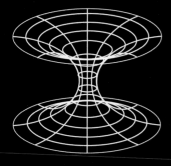

What if you could find a window into another part of the universe, then step through it onto the surface of another planet?

- Worm holes are very tiny, much smaller than an atom! We'd have to find a way to make them bigger.

- Worm holes don't stay open very long! We'd have to find a way to keep them from closing up on us.

- Worm holes are very hard to find. And if we did find them, who says they'd lead to a place we wanted to go? We'd have to find a way to move them to suit our travel plans!

QuickBlast

The Space Explorer's Guide to Time Travel

On page 29, you learned about one way to travel into the future—by zooming out into space at nearly light speed, so your clock would run slower compared to the clocks you left behind on Earth. When you returned to Earth, you'd be in the future! Check out the Space U web site at www.scholastic.com/space to explore this kind of time travel!

But what about traveling to the *past*? Well, that's a little more complicated. Some physicists think that travel to the past might turn out to be impossible, because a time traveler could mess up the series of events that brought him into existence in the first place!

For example, think about this problem:

- What if you traveled to the past and prevented your parents from meeting? How would you have been born? Would you pop out of existence right then and there?

Think about how *you* would resolve this problem, and then turn to page 48 to see what some physicists think!

>> 48

Well, that's all for me and *The Case of Space and Time*. I'll be heading through this worm hole now to page 48. See you there!

What if we told you that all the stars and planets that make up the universe you know are only a tiny part of what's actually out there—and the rest is invisible? That's what astronomers have discovered!

IN THE DARK

Scientists have found that somewhere around 85 percent of the mass in the universe is made up of matter we can't see. What *is* this invisible stuff? No one knows!

The search is on to find this missing mass, which is called *dark matter* because it doesn't give off any light. But how do we *know* this dark matter exists? And how are we supposed to figure out exactly what it is, if we can't see or detect it? Let's talk to an expert....

Meet Detective Ivana B. Hidden

Hello, cadet, I'm Ivana B. Hidden, lead detective on *The Case of the Missing Matter*. I may be dark and mysterious, but I'll make sure that *you're* not left in the dark! On the next few pages, I'll guide you through the evidence in this case—and then you'll have a chance to check out a line-up of dark matter suspects on page 43!

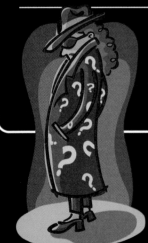

The mass we can see when we look at galaxies is the bright stuff, like stars. From what you can see in the galaxy on the right, it appears that most of the mass is in the center of the galaxy (where it's brightest). There seems to be less and less mass around the galaxy's edges. Is that really the case? Read on to find out!

Clue #1
Whirling Wonders

How did scientists realize that dark matter was out there? A big clue came from watching galaxies whirl!

Planets orbit stars, stars orbit around the centers of galaxies, and galaxies orbit around each other in clusters. This is all due to *gravity*. Scientists have understood gravity for hundreds of years and can find out how much mass is in a star just by observing how long it takes a planet to orbit around it. We also know how much mass is in our Milky Way Galaxy by watching how long it takes our Sun to orbit around the galaxy's center.

Surprising Spinning

When astronomer Vera Rubin watched galaxies, she expected to see that the stars orbiting near the bright centers of the galaxies (where we can see lots of mass) would move much faster than the stars near the dark edges. That's how orbits in solar systems work—in our solar system, for example, Mercury orbits much faster than faraway Pluto.

Vera Rubin

But instead, Rubin noticed something very odd—the outer stars were orbiting much faster than expected. This meant that the outer regions of galaxies had a whole lot more mass than astronomers could actually see!

Astronomer Frank Zwicky noticed the same thing happening to galaxies themselves: Galaxies in the Coma cluster were orbiting around each other much faster than they should have been, based on the amount of bright (shining) mass we see.

What causes these high-speed orbits? If the matter scientists *see* isn't enough to create these orbits, then...

...there must be matter we *can't* see!

This cluster might have luster... but is that all that matters? I think not!

This was one of the first clues that dark matter exists. Turn the page to find *another* clue!

The galaxies in this cluster orbit around each other much faster than astronomers calculate based on the amount of visible mass they detect.

Using the Hubble Space Telescope to look at distant superclusters of galaxies, scientists have been able to see the effects of dark matter by measuring an effect called *gravitational lensing*.

The Hubble Space Telescope

The Lensing of Light

A lens bends light—when you look through a telescope, you're seeing objects magnified because of the way light bends when it passes through the scope's lenses. An object with a lot of gravity can bend light, too. On page 35, you saw how starlight bends around the space-time warp created by the Sun. This same effect happens on a larger scale when light from distant galaxies bends around a massive galaxy cluster. And just like your telescope lens magnifies images, these distant galaxies are magnified, too!

Cluster Clues

In images like the one below, we can see light getting bent around clusters of galaxies. Scientists can determine how much matter it would take to bend the light like this, and every time, the amount of visible matter is not enough to do the job.

That's what gave astronomers another clue that there's more matter out there than meets the eye! If the matter astronomers can see in galaxies isn't enough to bend light...

...then most of the matter in galaxies must be *dark matter!*

So, if all our clues tell us that dark matter *exists*, then the next question is: What's it made of? Check out the next page!

Check out a line-up of my top suspects!

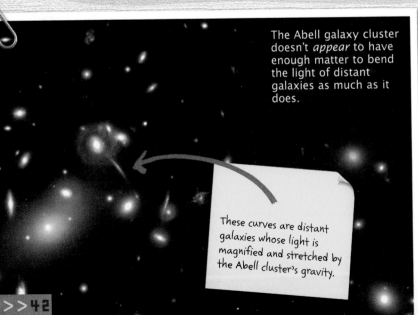

The Abell galaxy cluster doesn't *appear* to have enough matter to bend the light of distant galaxies as much as it does.

These curves are distant galaxies whose light is magnified and stretched by the Abell cluster's gravity.

THE DARK MATTER SUSPECTS!

Any of the following suspects could be the missing matter. One or all of them might be guilty. Until we know, the search is on to catch them!

THE "WIMP" GANG

These Weakly Interacting Massive Particles (WIMPs) are very hard to find because they're so tiny—even smaller than a proton or neutron! They're very shy and don't like to interact with any other particles. Even though they're small, they have mass (that's why they're called "massive"), so they can create gravity. If there are a whole lot of them, then all their tiny masses could add up to a large amount of the missing mass!

Here are just a few of the most notorious WIMPs:

Axions: These shy particles have never been observed, but since so many of them were made in the early universe, we might find them someday.

Wimpzillas: The name is no joke—these WIMPs are the heavyweights of the gang. They've not yet been detected, but they're very strong contenders for the missing mass title!

Neutralinos: These might be the lightest neutral particles in the group, but they're the leading suspects for dark matter. This nice and stable particle is the partner of the photon, the carrier of light.

Neutrinos: Their name means "little neutral ones," and there are different kinds—some fairly heavy, and some with almost no mass at all.

THE "MACHO" GANG

These Massive Compact Halo Objects (MACHOs) are a very different group. They're all large and very massive, but they don't give off light, so they're really hard to find.

Members include:

Neutron Stars: These small, spinning stars are often left behind after massive stars die in supernova explosions. They send out pulses of light, but if the pulses aren't aimed our way, we won't detect them!

Black Holes: All alone in space, a black hole can be very massive and yet very hard to find.

Black Dwarfs: When lower-mass stars burn out, they become black dwarfs. Good luck spotting *these* dark lumps with a telescope!

Brown Dwarfs: These small wannabe stars didn't have enough mass to make it as real stars. They're very dim and hard to see with a telescope.

WHO WILL YOU NAB?

Which gang do *you* think is the most likely suspect in *The Case of the Missing Matter*? Log on to the

Space U web site (www.scholastic.com/space) to cast your vote! You can also turn the page to meet a scientist who studies dark matter. Find out which gang he suspects!

That's all for now, cadet—but if you liked poking around in the dark, head over to page 45 to learn about dark *energy* in *The Case of the Cosmic Conclusion!*

Dr. Rocky Kolb

COSMOLOGIST

Now that you've investigated *The Case of the Missing Matter*, meet a scientist who's hot on the trail of dark matter suspects!

Dr. Rocky Kolb is a cosmologist at the Fermi National Accelerator Laboratory (Fermilab) in Illinois and a professor of astronomy and astrophysics at the University of Chicago.

Question: What made you want to become a cosmologist?

Answer: The big money! No, really...I wanted to be a cosmologist because the questions that cosmologists try to answer are very simple and fundamental. I can't remember ever wanting to be anything else. When I was a child, I read books about astronomy and space, and I was excited about the cosmic questions.

Q: Why are you interested in dark matter?

A: The riddle of dark matter is one of the basic questions of cosmology. For thousands of years people have asked, "What is the universe made of?" We now know that most of the mass of the universe is dark matter, but what exactly *is* the dark matter? Clues to its identity are all over the universe. We have to piece these clues together to solve the riddle of what the universe is made of.

Q: What kinds of tools do you use in your search for dark matter?

A: Astronomers and cosmologists use large telescopes, satellites, particle accelerators, and detectors deep underground as their tools in the search for dark matter. I use the most powerful tool available: the human imagination.

Q: What do *you* think dark matter is? MACHOs, WIMPs, or maybe something else that we haven't found yet?

A: I think dark matter is a particle that has not yet been discovered—a "fossil" particle produced in the very early moments of the Big Bang when the universe was a hot "soup" or fog of particles. There are many possible fossil particles. My favorite is one called the wimpzilla—a really, really heavy WIMP.

Q: If any of the kids reading this grow up to become cosmologists, what do you think they might be studying?

A: Dark matter is *our* cosmic question. The kids growing up now will answer all of our cosmic questions, and more importantly, they will develop cosmic questions of their very own. Remember, answering a big question usually leads to an even *more* interesting question!

Dr. Kolb stands beside a chalkboard with a stuffed-animal pal, whose name *also* happens to be Rocky!

Part 4: The Case of the Cosmic Conclusion

As you saw in *The Case of the Big Bang*, the universe is expanding. But did you know that it's *accelerating*? It's true—the universe's growth rate is getting faster and faster over time.

But what could be causing this acceleration, and what does it mean for the future of the universe? Big questions like these are the focus of your next case: *The Case of the Cosmic Conclusion!*

Meet Detective Barry Distant

Hi there, cadet, I'm detective Barry Distant! I keep a close eye on our expanding universe to predict what will happen to it in the very distant future. But don't keep your distance from me—because I'll give you a sneak peek into the future on the next page!

KEPT IN THE DARK

Astronomers can't see anything that could make the universe expand faster and faster—so the cause of this acceleration must be invisible! Scientists call the invisible energy that pushes the universe outward *dark energy*.

This dark energy competes with gravity—gravity pulls matter together, and dark energy pushes matter apart. Dark energy fills empty space, and, like dark matter, we don't know what it is! We just know it pushes outward, like your puffs of air do when you blow up a balloon.

As the universe expands, matter gets farther and farther apart, so gravity becomes less and less of a match for dark energy's outward push. That makes the universe accelerate! What will happen in the future if this acceleration continues? Turn the page to find out!

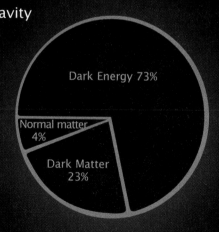

Dark Energy 73%

Normal matter 4%

Dark Matter 23%

This chart shows you what makes up the universe. "Normal matter" includes stars, planets, people, and everything else you see around you!

The
FUTURE
of the
UNIVERSE
As We Now See It

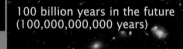

The timeline below shows you the future of the universe *if* the acceleration continues at its current rate. The acceleration could change, or the future of the universe could play out in a completely different way. We can't say for sure!

These events might sound scary, but don't worry, cadet—they're billions and trillions of years away. Just check out all the zeroes at the end of the timeline— that's more than a *googol* (a googol has 100 zeroes)!

---

3 billion years in the future (3,000,000,000 years)

5 billion years in the future (5,000,000,000 years)

100 billion years in the future (100,000,000,000 years)

Galactic Collision

As you learned on page 19, galaxies within a cluster can crash into each other, thanks to their strong gravity—and that's what our Milky Way has to look forward to!

In about 3 billion years, the Milky Way will collide with the Andromeda Galaxy. The two galaxies might merge into one large galaxy, or they could rip each other apart and fling some of their stars out into intergalactic space.

The Sun's Slow End

In a few billion years, the Sun will run low on hydrogen in its core. As its outer layers puff out and cool, it will become a red giant. After the Sun finally exhausts all its fuel (about 5 billion years from now), it will slowly cool as a white dwarf.

And what about the Earth? Well, the Earth will be (gasp!) cooked and then probably swallowed by the swelling Sun. But before you panic, remember that this is billions of years in the future!

Runaway Galaxies

As the cosmic expansion continues to speed up, only the galaxies in our Local Group will stay near the Milky Way because of gravity—all the other galaxies in the universe will spread so far away that they won't be visible, even with really powerful telescopes.

Tools on the Cosmic Horizon

All of this stuff is *way* far off in the future—so what can you expect in *your* lifetime? Be on the lookout for far-out discoveries about the mysterious ways the universe works!

Lots more clues are headed our way about dark energy, dark matter, and other cosmic cases, thanks to these upcoming satellites and experiments:

- **Laser Interferometer Space Antenna (LISA):** This satellite will look for ripples in the fabric of space-time that will tell us more about the Big Bang and black holes.

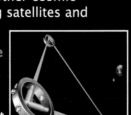

- **Large Hadron Collider (LHC):** This particle collider will search for the smallest particles of matter to help researchers understand what the early universe might have been like.

- **James Webb Space Telescope:** Looking for the nature and amount of dark matter in the universe is just one goal of this space telescope, which is scheduled to replace the Hubble Space Telescope in 2011.

- **Cryogenic Dark Matter Search (CDMS):** Remember the WIMPs from page 43— some of the suspects in *The Case of the Missing Matter*? This experiment will search for WIMPs using detectors located deep underground in a mine in Minnesota. Why underground? Because the only things that can go through the ground and reach the detectors are particles that don't interact with matter (that's why the "WI" in WIMP stands for "Weakly Interacting")!

---

1 trillion years in the future (1,000,000,000,000 years)

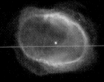

A planetary nebula, the remains of a dying star

Ten trillion trillion trillion years in the future

(10,000,000,000,000,000,000, 000,000,000,000,000,000 years!)

10 thousand trillion trillion trillion trillion trillion trillion trillion years in the future

(10,000,000,000,000,000,000,000 ,000,000,000,000,000,000,000, 000,000,000,000,000,000,000, 000,000,000,000,000,000,000, 000,000,000,000,000 years!)

The End of the Stellar Era

In about a *trillion* years, most of the stars will have run out of gas, and the stellar era that we are currently in will come to an end. Since most of the matter in the universe will be bound up in dead stars and black holes, there will be no more new gas and dust to form baby stars.

The Degenerate Era

The only light in the universe at this point will be from old, cooling stars. As the stars cool down, eventually even the protons that make up their atoms will decay into energy. Finally, there will be no stars left.

The Black Hole Era

When all the protons in the universe have decayed into energy, the only thing left will be black holes. Slowly, the black holes will disappear, and this era will end.

The Dark Era

Case NOT Closed!

So, cadet, another Space U adventure is about to conclude, but that doesn't mean that your cosmic cases are closed!

All the detectives at Space U hope that your training has been a mind-EXPANDING experience. You've learned some of the clues that tell us the story of the universe, but there are so many more clues to be found!

So, keep asking your cosmic questions, cadet! Who knows—one day you might find your very own piece of the cosmic puzzle!

THE ANSWER STATION

Page 30: Plane Old Time!

C) The clock on the airplane was a tiny fraction of a second behind the one on the ground (about 40 *billionths* of a second).

Page 39: The Space Explorer's Guide to Time Travel

There are lots of ways you could approach this problem (or "paradox"). But here are two:

1) Maybe there is no way you could prevent your parents from meeting. Maybe, despite all of your efforts, you would not be able to disrupt the chain of events that brought you into being. Your parents would still find a way to meet—or maybe your efforts to keep them apart would actually end up bringing them together!

2) Or, maybe there are multiple universes. By traveling back into time, you could be entering a whole new universe. It would *seem* like your universe, but really it would be a copy. So, if you changed history, it wouldn't affect *your* past. Strange, huh?

There is no right answer here, cadet! What do *you* think?